SCIENCE WORKSHOP

LIGHT
COLOR, & LENSES

Pam Robson

FRANKLIN WATTS
NEW YORK CHICAGO LONDON TORONTO SYDNEY

Design	David West
	Children's Book Design
Designer	Steve Woosnam-Savage
Editor	Suzanne Melia
Picture Researcher	Emma Krikler
Illustrators	Ian Moores
	Ian Thompson
Consultant	Geoff Leyland

© Aladdin Books Ltd 1992

First published in
the United States in 1993 by
Gloucester Press
95 Madison Avenue
New York, NY10016

Library of Congress Cataloging-in-Publication Data

Robson, Pam.
    Light, color, and lenses / Pam Robson
        p.   cm. — (Science workshop)
    Includes index.
    Summary: Suggests projects for exploring the
properties of light and how it can be refracted,
reflected, and diffracted.
    ISBN 0-531-17407-7
    1. Light—Juvenile literature. 2. Light—
Experiments—Juvenile literature. [1. Light—
Experiments. 2. Experiments.] I. Title. II. Series.
QC360.R6   1993
535'.078—dc20
92-37097   CIP   AC

CONTENTS

THE WORKSHOP	4
LIGHT AND SHADOW	6
WHAT IS LIGHT?	8
SUNLIGHT	10
THE EYE	12
REFLECTION	14
CURVED MIRRORS	16
REFRACTION	18
LENSES	20
THE SPECTRUM	22
COLORED LIGHT	24
PIGMENTS	26
MOVING PICTURES	28
CONCENTRATED LIGHT	30
INDEX/GLOSSARY	32

PHOTOCREDITS
All the photographs in this book are by Roger
Vlitos apart from pages; 10: Mary Evans
Picture Library; 12 top, 14 top left, 20 top
and 22 top: Science Photo Library; 16 top:
Frank Spooner Pictures; 28 top: British Film
Institute, London; 30: STL Designs.

INTRODUCTION

Light is all around us. Light is color and it enables us to see. It creates rainbows and makes color television possible. It can camouflage and it can warn of dangers. Light allows artists to use color to create works of art. The sun is our most important source of natural light. Without the sun, there would be no light, and so no life on Earth. Sunlight enables plants to grow. All of our food comes from plants or the animals that eat plants. Plants also give off oxygen which is essential for us to breathe. Fire was the first manmade light source. Later, candles, oil-lamps, gas lights, and electric lights were developed. Today, we can use the sun's rays to heat our homes and to create artificial light. Technology has conquered darkness, but the earth's nonrenewable sources of energy, such as coal and oil, are now running out. Light draws our attention to things of importance – it can illuminate, highlight or spotlight. It allows us to see objects as far away as stars and as small as specks of dust. The smallest atom has become visible because of light, and we have begun to understand the mysteries of our universe.

Why It Works explaining the science ideas

Bright Ideas for further projects

Introduction

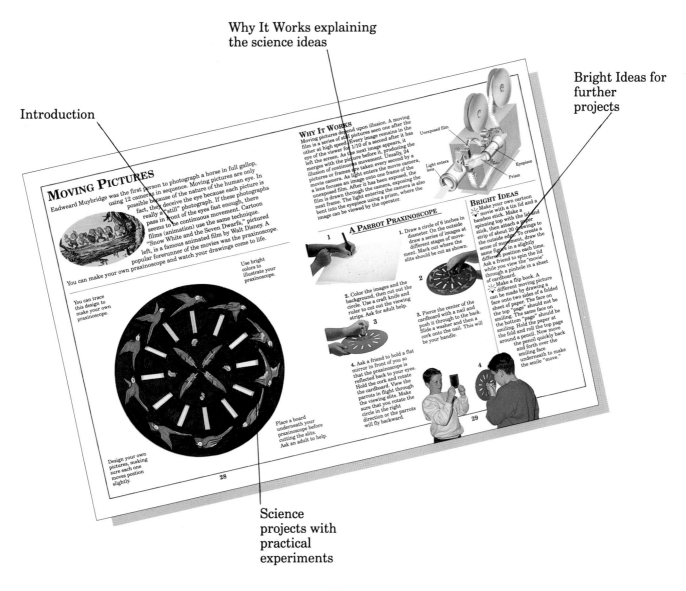

Science projects with practical experiments

THE WORKSHOP

A science workshop is a place to test ideas, perform experiments, and make discoveries. To prove many scientific facts, you don't need a lot of fancy equipment. In fact, everything you need for a basic workshop can be found around your home or school. Read through these pages, and then use your imagination to add to your "home laboratory." Make sure that you are aware of relevant safety rules, and show concern for the environment. A science experiment is an activity that involves the use of certain basic rules to test a hypothesis. A qualitative approach involves observation. A quantitative approach involves measurement. Remember, one of the keys to being a creative scientist is to keep experimenting. This means experimenting with equipment as well as with ideas to give you the most accurate results. In this way you will build up your workshop as you go along.

MAKING MODELS

Before you begin, read through all the steps. Then make a list of the things you need and gather them together. Next, think about the project so that you have a clear idea of what you are about to do. Finally, take your time in putting the pieces together. You will find that your projects work best if you wait while glue or paint dries. If something goes wrong, retrace your steps. And, if you can't fix it, start over again. Every scientist makes mistakes, but the best ones know when to begin again!

GENERAL TIPS

There are at least two parts to every experiment: experimenting with materials and testing a science "fact." If you don't have all the materials, experiment with others instead. For example, if you can't find any tracing paper, use grease-proof wax paper instead. Once you've finished experimenting, read your notes thoroughly and think about what happened, evaluating your measurements and observations. See what conclusions you can draw from your results.

SAFETY WARNINGS

Make sure that an adult knows what you are doing at all times. Concentrating sunlight through a lens can be dangerous. Ask an adult to do this for you. In the experiments that use an artificial light source, always use a flashlight with two D batteries. Never use electrical outlets. Always be careful with scissors. If you spill any water, wipe it up right away. Slippery surfaces are dangerous. Clean up after you have finished.

EXPERIMENTING

Always conduct a "fair test." This means changing one thing at a time for each stage of an experiment. In this way you can always tell which change caused a different result. As you go along, record what you see. Ask questions such as "why?," "how?," and "what if?" Then test your model and write down the answers you come up with. Compare your results to those of your class-mates or friends.

LIGHT AND SHADOW

On the morning of July 11, 1991, the shadow of the moon stretched for 100 miles across Hawaii and the mainland of the United States during a solar eclipse. A solar eclipse happens when the moon lies directly between the earth and the sun, preventing light from reaching the earth. Light radiates (spreads out) in all directions from its source. Light is made up of tiny particles of energy, called photons. These travel in small waves and move in straight lines, called rays. Because light cannot bend around objects, shadows form behind objects. For centuries, time has been calculated using shadows. A sundial is a clock that uses shadows to tell the time.

SHADOW SCENE

1. You will need sheets of stiff, dark-colored oak tag, paper fasteners, tracing paper, glue, and straws. Your light source may be a flashlight or a penlight. Draw the characters on the oak tag, as shown, leaving the body separate from the limbs. The weapons are cut out attached to the hands, the shield is cut out separately.

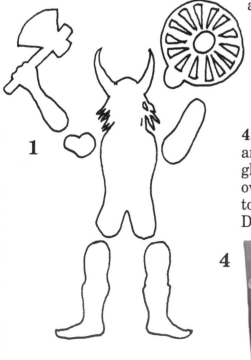

2. Join the limbs to the body with the paper fasteners to make them movable. Attach the shield in the same way.

3. Attach two plastic straws to the feet, as shown here. This allows you to control the puppet's movements.

4. Cut a semicircle out of another sheet of oak tag, and glue a piece of tracing paper over the hole. Make supports to keep the screen upright. Decorate the front.

BRIGHT IDEAS

-☀- Make a sundial like the
-☀- one shown here. Use a
watch to check the time each
hour and mark where the
shadows fall. The shadows
will not be the same length
all year around.

-☀- Substitute the
-☀- light for your
shadow theater for
a more powerful one.
What do you notice about
the silhouettes now?

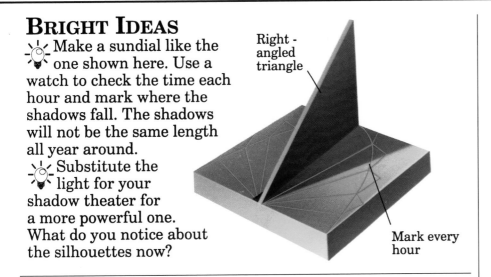

Right-angled triangle

Mark every hour

5. Cut out scenery to stand
behind the screen. Someone
behind the screen must
manipulate the puppets while
someone else directs the light
source on to them.

WHY IT WORKS

Shadow is the absence of
light. A shadow forms on a
surface when light rays are
obstructed by an opaque
object. The cardboard
shadow puppets are opaque.
This means light cannot pass
through them. The nature of
the shadow depends upon
the size and position of both
the light source and the
object. The closer the light to
the object, the larger the
shadow.

Because light travels in a
straight line, it cannot turn
corners. A very small source
of light – a point source like
a pinhole – creates a sharp
shadow that is equally dark
all over. The presence of an
opaque object – like the
moon in the path of the sun
– creates the dark shadow
that we call an eclipse. A
large or extended source of
light creates a larger shadow
with a central dark region.
The darker part of the
shadow with a sharp edge is
called the umbra. The paler,
fuzzy part of the shadow
encircling it is the
penumbra.

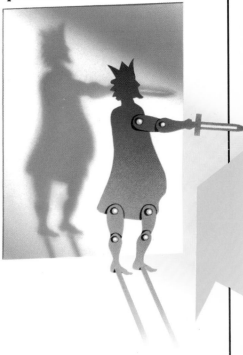

WHAT IS LIGHT?

Natural sunlight contains lots of different types of light, including infrared rays and ultraviolet rays. These are invisible to our eyes. Light travels very fast, much faster than anything else in the universe. It can travel through air and other transparent substances. Visible light cannot travel through opaque materials like cardboard. Glass is opaque to ultraviolet light, which is invisible. Visible and invisible light have different wavelengths. White light is made up of all the colors you can see in a rainbow (see pages 22/23). Colored glass or paper filters white light to create stunning effects. A famous stained-glass window is the rose window in the Notre Dame Cathedral in Paris.

WHY IT WORKS

We see an object only if light from it enters our eyes. A totally transparent object is invisible. Clean air is transparent because light passes through it. It does not bounce off it. A translucent object allows some light to pass through it and it scatters the rest – a cloud is translucent. An opaque object scatters all light – a book is opaque. Luminous objects like the sun, make their own light. Nonluminous objects scatter light from a luminous source. For example, the moon is illuminated by the sun. Pieces of colored plastic or glass that only allow one color of light to pass through them are called filters. Clear, red glass or plastic allows all the red light to pass through. Translucent red glass does not produce such an intense color.

Clear red

Translucent red

COLORFUL WINDOWS

1. You will need black oak tag, colored tissue paper, glue, and felt-tip pens.

1

2. On the sheet of black oak tag, design your stained-glass window and cut out each section as shown. Cut pieces of colored tissue for your window, and use felt-tip pens to color in white tissue. Glue them in place as shown.

2

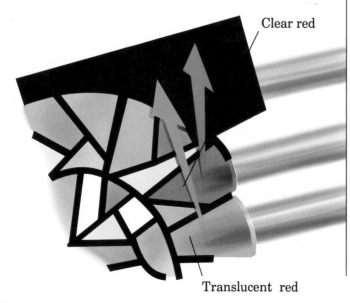

BRIGHT IDEAS

☀ Suspend a sheet of bubble wrap so that you can walk around it. Darken the room and project a picture onto it using a slide projector. Bubble wrap is translucent – you can view the picture from both sides.

☀ Collect a variety of materials. Shine a light from behind each and ask someone to observe whether they are opaque, transparent, or translucent. See what kind of shadow is created.

3

3. Finally, secure the whole window, and place it inside a real window. When sunlight filters through, you will notice the different amounts and colors of light that pass through.

SUNLIGHT

The sun is a star that gives us light and heat energy. The sun is about 93 million miles from the earth. All plants grow toward the sun. If you see a field of sunflowers, like the one pictured here, you will notice that they all face the same way, toward the sun. Plants use the sun's energy to make their own food. This energy is trapped by the green chlorophyll in a plant's leaves. During a process called photosynthesis, oxygen is released into the air as the sunlight is used to convert nutrients from the soil into food. The Greek word "photo" means light. Bioethanol is a fuel made by fermenting the food produced by plants like wheat. One day it could replace gasoline.

LEAVES

1. Half fill a shallow container with soil and scatter cress seeds on the top. Keep the soil moist and place the tray in a sunny position. Leave it until the seeds sprout.

3. Leave the tray in its sunny position. You may have to wait as long as two weeks. Keep the soil moist while the cress is growing.

3

1

2. Cut out your initials from some cardboard, and place it over the seedlings. Make sure the sunlight cannot reach the plants beneath.

4

2

4. During this growing time do not remove the cardboard. You may want to turn the tray occasionally to allow an equal amount of light to reach every part of the tray.

5. When you observe that the cress is fully grown, remove the cardboard. You should be able to see your initials in the seedlings. They will be a much darker green than the rest of the cress, where the light could not reach.

WHY IT WORKS

Sunlight is used by plants to convert nutrients from the soil into chemical energy for growth. When the leaves are covered, sunlight cannot be absorbed. No food can be manufactured inside the plant. Plants absorb carbon dioxide and water. These are converted by the green chlorophyll in the leaves into oxygen and simple sugars. The sugars are converted into food for the plant while the remaining oxygen and water is released into the air through small holes called stomata. These are located on the underside of the leaves. This process is called photosynthesis.

Sunlight

Carbon dioxide
absorbed

Water
absorbed

Oxygen
and water
released

BRIGHT IDEAS

Starch is produced when leaves photosynthesize. You can test for starch. Ask an adult to help you. Remove some cress from different parts of the tray and soak them in rubbing alcohol to remove any green chlorophyll. Then place them on a clean surface and put drops of dilute iodine on the surface of each. Where starch is present, the leaves will turn blue, where there is no starch they will turn brown.

Plants always grow toward the sun. This is called phototropism. Plant a seedling in a pot and place it in a shoe box. Place a hole at one end of the box for the light to enter. The shoot will appear through the hole.

5

THE EYE

You see an object when light is reflected from it into your eyes. The eye is like a very small, but accurate, camera. The lens that is inside the eye and the cornea, which covers the colored iris, act together as the focusing apparatus. Light bounces off the object in view and travels in straight lines to the eye. An upside-down image is formed on the retina at the back of the eye. A nerve called the optic nerve carries a message to the brain, where the image is seen right-side up. In the dark, the pupil widens to allow more light to enter the eye. This is why nocturnal animals often have large eyes. A blind person may use other senses, such as touch, for "seeing."

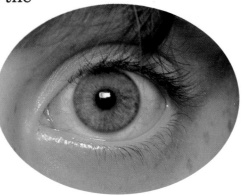

5

PINHOLE CAMERA

1

1. You will need a rectangular cardboard box, a cardboard tube, tracing paper, oak tag and a large rubber band. Position the cardboard tube at one end of the box and draw a circle around it. Cut out the circle. At the other end of the box, make a small viewing hole.

2. Cover one end of the cardboard tube with tracing paper and secure it in place with a rubber band. Cover the other end with an oak tag circle, making sure that no light can enter. Make one small pinhole in the center.

2

3. Insert the tube inside the box with the tracing paper – covered end going in first. Leave the other end sticking out to look like the lens of your camera. Secure it in place with masking tape.

4. Add a decorative button for the top of the camera, as shown, and paint it brightly. Make sure that the only way light can enter the camera is through the pinhole in the front. Your eye will cover the viewing hole at the back.

3

4

5. Hold the finished camera up to your eye, and direct it toward an object near a window. As light rays from the object enter through the pinhole in the front of the camera, you can view an image of it on the circle of tracing paper.

WHY IT WORKS

There is a lens, made of a soft, jellolike substance, in each of your eyes. In the pinhole camera, the pinhole acts as the lens. The inverted (upside-down) image it creates is produced when one ray of light from each point of the object passes through the pinhole and falls onto the screen. A two-dimensional image is formed. The pinhole camera works only because light travels in straight lines. The size of the image depends on the distance of the object from the pinhole and the distance of the pinhole from the screen.

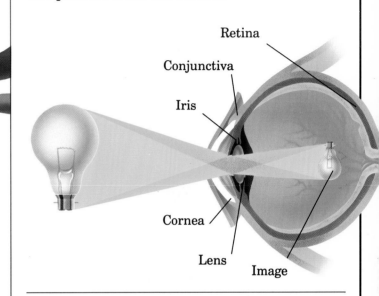

Retina

Conjunctiva

Iris

Cornea

Lens

Image

BRIGHT IDEAS

🔦 Move the pinhole camera closer to the object. What can you see now?

🔦 As both eyes see a slightly different picture of an object, it is possible to create optical illusions. See if the two bars are the same distance apart all the way along. What about the two lines? Are they the same length? Are the yellow circles the same size?

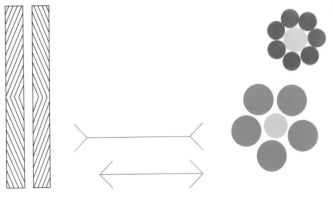

13

REFLECTION

When light rays hit a surface, they bounce off again, like a ball bouncing off a wall. This is called reflection. The way light behaves when it hits a reflective surface is used by people and animals to see more clearly. Cats have eyes designed to reflect as much light as possible, because they need to see in the dark. Inside high-quality periscopes on board submarines, prisms (blocks of glass) are used to bend beams of light around corners, making objects at the surface visible. Light can be made to reflect off a surface. Mirrors can also be used inside a periscope. Make your own periscope and let nothing spoil your view!

UP PERISCOPE!

1

1. Use a ruler and pencil to measure and draw a plan of your periscope like the one shown here. Cut out the two windows and the four slits. Fold along the dotted lines.

2

2. Take two flat mirrors of the same size and put masking tape around the edges. These should be slightly wider than the periscope.

4. Slide the mirrors into the slits so that the reflecting faces are opposite each other. The edges of the mirrors will protrude from the periscope case. Make sure that they are secure. If they are not, they may slide out and break.

3. Use glue or colored masking tape to stick down the folded sides and flaps. Paint the outside of your periscope.

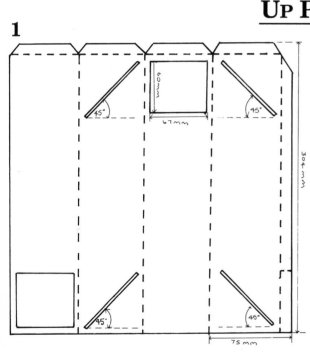

3

4

WHY IT WORKS

Light is reflected at the same angle as it hits an object, but in the opposite direction. The top mirror of the periscope is positioned to reflect light from the object downward to the other mirror. The bottom mirror is at the same angle as the top one and reflects the beam out of the periscope and into the eye.

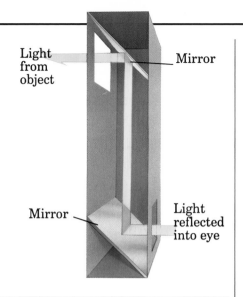

Light from object

Mirror

Mirror

Light reflected into eye

5. Use your periscope to view over an obstruction such as a fence or wall. Look into the bottom mirror to see what is hidden there. Notice what happens when you hold the periscope sideways. Try to look around corners as well.

BRIGHT IDEAS

With three mirrors arranged in a triangular pattern, you can make a kaleidoscope. Cover one end with tracing paper and the other with cardboard. Make a hole in the oak tag to see through, and drop colored paper inside. Point the end toward a light source. Use materials of different colors.

Write a message on paper and look at it in a mirror. You can turn a message into code by standing a mirror vertically above it and copying the image in the mirror. It can only be decoded with another mirror because it is upside down and back to front.

5

CURVED MIRRORS

The reflecting telescope, developed by Sir Isaac Newton (1642 –1727), uses two mirrors to reflect light through a small lens. In 1781, William Herschel became the first scientist to see the planet Uranus using a reflecting telescope. Today, large telescopes like the one pictured here, use huge, curved mirrors to produce real images of distant stars. In an amusement park, the house of mirrors uses curved mirrors to create weird distortions. Build your own simple reflector telescope and have a closer look at the moon.

MAN IN THE MOON

1. To make a reflecting "telescope" you will need a concave mirror on a stand, a convex lens or a magnifying glass, and a flat mirror.

1

2. Mount the flat mirror on stiff cardboard so that it can be held without covering the image formed in it. Polish both mirrors to ensure a sharp, well-defined image in each.

2

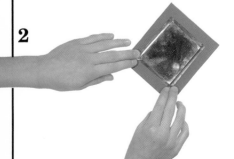

4

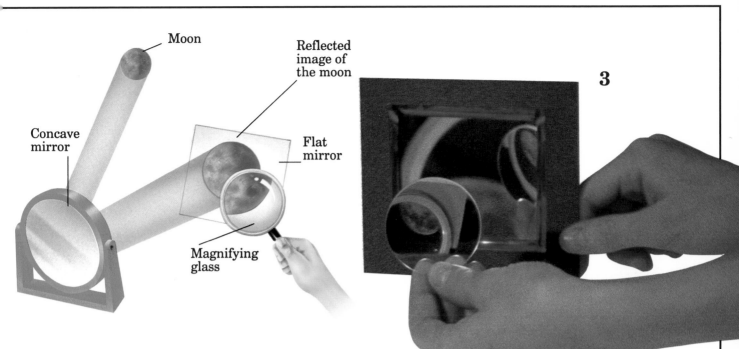

Moon

Reflected image of the moon

Concave mirror

Flat mirror

Magnifying glass

3. This project is best attempted on a clear night when there is a full moon. Place the concave mirror in a window so that it points toward the moon. Position the flat mirror so that the image of the moon in the concave mirror is reflected into it.

4. Now look at the moon's image in the flat mirror through the convex lens. It will look much brighter. A magnifying glass can be used instead of a convex lens. Never look at the sun through a telescope; you may cause damage to your eyes. This project must only be attempted at night. Try to focus on a particular constellation of stars with your "telescope."

BRIGHT IDEAS

A simple way to see the difference between the images produced in concave and convex mirrors is to look into both sides of the bowl of a shiny, metal spoon. Look around you to find other examples of curved mirrors used in everyday life. Remember that any shiny surface behaves like a mirror. Make two lists, one for concave and one for convex. Look in the side of a cool shiny kettle. Notice how a light from a car's headlights is reflected. Find a safe place to stand beside a stationary car and observe your reflection in the curved walls of the lights.

WHY IT WORKS

A concave mirror (left) curves inward. When light hits the mirror, the light rays converge (move closer together). A convex mirror (right) curves outward, causing the light rays to diverge (move farther apart).

In this simple reflecting telescope, the concave mirror reflects the light and brings it in focus. The beam then reflects onto a small, flat mirror where the image can be magnified with a lens or magnifying glass.

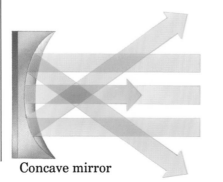

Concave mirror

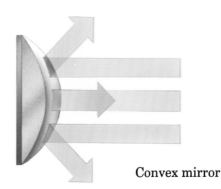

Convex mirror

REFRACTION

A mirror reflects light, a lens refracts (bends) light. Light waves are refracted as they pass through a transparent substance like a glass lens. Light also refracts as it passes from one substance to another, such as from air to water. When light rays are refracted, objects may appear closer or farther away than they really are. Lenses can be used to make things look bigger. The microscope was invented by Robert Hooke in about 1665. One of the first things he viewed through it was a hair louse clinging to a human hair. Today, microscopes range from a small pocket version, to a powerful electron microscope, like the one pictured here. This one can magnify objects by 1 million times their size.

WHY IT WORKS

There are two types of lens – convex and concave. A convex lens bulges out at the center, a concave lens is thinner. In a concave lens the light rays diverge (move apart) – the image appears smaller. In a convex lens, light rays converge (move closer) – the image seen may appear larger. The water drop in the simple microscope acts as a convex lens. The light is reflected from the mirror, through the object. The light is then magnified as it passes through the drop of water and into the eye.

Concave lens

Convex lens

MAKE A MICROSCOPE

1. To make a microscope you will need a see-through plastic bottle, a small, flat mirror, scissors and a drop of water. First cut the top off the bottle and cut a strip 1-2 in wide and 5-6 in long from each side.

2. Use one of these strips as a slide on which the object to be viewed will be positioned. The second strip will act as a lens holder for the drop of water. The object will be viewed here, through the drop of water.

3. Insert the ends of one strip through the slits in the sides. Leave room for the slide holding the object to be held underneath. A drop of water will be balanced on the top strip.

4. Place the mirror, reflecting face-up, in the base of the container. On top of the slide, place the object to be viewed. Look down through the drop of water to the object. It will appear to be magnified.

BRIGHT IDEAS

Collect a variety of interesting objects, such as leaves, grains of wheat, or hairs to look at through a magnifying glass. Look at the shape of the lens. Make drawings of what you see through the lens. Hold a convex lens between the magnifying glass and an object. You have made a simple microscope.

Look through a plain glass marble at a small object of interest – what do you notice? Now hold a magnifying glass vertically between a sheet of white paper and a window when the sun is shining (never look directly at the sun). Focus on an object in the window. What do you notice about the image focused on the paper?

Water also refracts light. Half fill a transparent beaker with salt solution. Carefully pour pure water on to the top, using the back of a spoon so that the two do not mix. Place a pencil upright in the beaker. It will appear to be broken in two places.

LENSES

It is generally accepted that the refracting telescope, invented in 1608 by a Dutch eyeglass-maker, Hans Lippersahey, was the first telescope to be invented. By 1610, Galileo Galilei was able to make a scientific study of the known universe using a refracting telescope. His observations challenged the popular belief that the earth was the center of the universe. Lenses are used in microscopes and telescopes. A telescope gives a close-up view of a distant object by producing an image of the object inside the telescope tube. The eye piece then magnifies the image. A refracting telescope uses a lens to form the image, not a mirror.

WHY IT WORKS

The large convex lens at the end of the telescope is called the object lens. It gathers light from the object being viewed. When light from the object strikes the lens, the rays are refracted and brought together to form a focal point. A small image is formed here. As light enters the eyepiece, the image is enlarged and appears closer. The image is also upside down. The telescope is focused by changing the distance between the object lens and the lens in the eyepiece.

In focus

Out of focus

IN FOCUS

1. Take a large cardboard tube and fit a convex lens into one end. This tube should be wide enough for another tube to fit inside.

2. Take the narrower tube and insert a plastic eyepiece into one end, using styrofoam to hold it in place. This eyepiece could be an empty film container with the end cut out.

3. Insert a small convex lens into one end of the eyepiece. This will be the end that you look through.

4. Push the narrow tube inside the wider tube, making sure that it slides smoothly in and out. Your telescope is now ready to use. Hold it up to your eye and point it at a distant object.

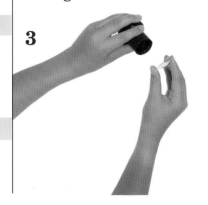

1

3

4

BRIGHT IDEAS

Adjust the telescope to focus on objects at various distances. Make another kind of refracting telescope using one convex and one concave lens instead of two convex lenses. Attach a thick concave lens upright with modeling clay at the end of a length of wood or plastic, marked off in inch divisions. Line it up with a distant object and ask a friend to position a thin convex lens along the wood until the object is in focus. Hold it in position with clay. How far apart are the lenses? Does the object appear upside down? Is it magnified? Repeat the exercise, looking at other distant objects. Place a second convex lens between the other two. Notice what effect this has on the image seen.

Ask an adult to concentrate sunlight onto a sheet of paper using a magnifying glass – do this outside. The convex lens concentrates the light rays at the center sufficiently to set the paper on fire. This can also happen using a concave mirror.

21

THE SPECTRUM

In 1666, Sir Isaac Newton used a prism (a triangular block of glass) to demonstrate how white light can be split up into lots of different colors. These colors are called the spectrum. With a second prism, he showed how white light could be re-formed by mixing the colors. Prisms can be used to make beams of light turn corners inside periscopes. The Frenchman, Augustin Fresnel, introduced the use of glass prisms to collect the light rays from a lighthouse into one powerful beam. When a light ray strikes a prism, light is refracted. Raindrops act as prisms under certain conditions, creating a rainbow across the sky. Try making your own rainbow.

BRIGHT IDEAS

Look all around you for examples of white light being split up – take particular notice of glass objects. You can learn the correct order of the colors in the spectrum and in a rainbow by using the initials of each color in a name like ROY G. BIV.

WHY IT WORKS

Water acts like a prism, splitting light into its different wavelengths and producing a spectrum of seven colors: red, orange, yellow, green, blue, indigo, and violet. The spectrum occurs because as the light is refracted (bent) by the water, each color is bent at different angles, splitting the white light into colors. Raindrops falling while the sun is shining can cause refraction and reflection of white light. Colored rays of light spread out across the sky to create the curved band of a rainbow.

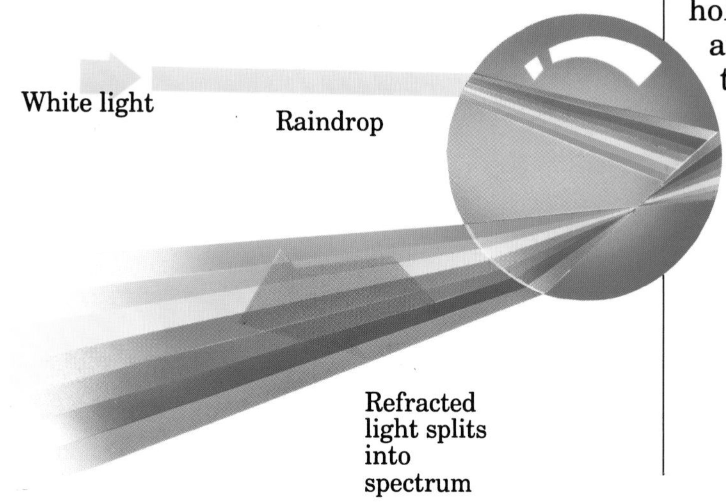

White light

Raindrop

Refracted light splits into spectrum

COLORS OF THE RAINBOW

1. Seal the edges of a mirror with tape. You will need two clips that are joined together like the ones shown here.

1

2. Half fill a glass container with water, and use the clips to hold it in the water at an angle. You may have to alter the angle later.

2

3. Find a piece of black oak tag, large enough to block out the light source completely. With sharp scissors, cut out one long, narrow strip as shown here. This will allow the passage of light from the light source to the mirror.

4. Rest the flat mirror at an angle in the container of water so that the light entering through the slit will strike it. Place a smaller piece of white oak tag beneath the slit in the black oak tag. Adjust the mirror's position until a rainbow appears.

3

4

COLORED LIGHT

Color and light are inseparable. The eye perceives color because of three sets of receptors called cones, one for each of the primary colors. All the colors seen on a television screen are made up from colored dots of the three primary colors. The color of an object will depend on which colors of the spectrum (see pages 22/23) it absorbs, and which it reflects. An object looks yellow because the yellow light rays are reflected into the eye, while the rest are absorbed. A black object absorbs all the colors of the spectrum, while a white object reflects them all.

BRIGHT IDEAS

Reconstitute white light by spinning a wheel like the one shown here. Color the wheel with colors of the spectrum and then spin it.

Make a hole in one end of a shoe box. Remove the lid and fill the box with objects of different colors. Make 2 or 3 cellophane covers, each a different color. Cover it with one of them, then shine a flashlight through the hole. Look through the cellophane. What color are the objects?

Colors of the spectrum

The colors disappear

SPOTLIGHTS

2. Attach these filters to three long, cardboard tubes. Make sure the filters cover the end of each tube completely.

2

WHY IT WORKS

We have discovered by splitting light that each color has a different wavelength. Mixing colored lights produces new colors by adding light of different wavelengths. Colored light mixtures are sometimes called additive color mixtures or color by addition. Luminous sources of light, like color televisions, combine colors by mixing very small dots of light. Black means the absence of light because there are no colors to mix together. When red, green, and blue lights are combined, white light is the result. A secondary color is an equal mixture of two primary colors. Red and green lights shining onto a white object will make it appear to be yellow. Any two colors of light that form white light when mixed are called complementary. Other colors are formed by mixing the primary colors in different proportions.

3. Place a large sheet of white oak tag on the floor in a darkened room. Three people need to hold the tubes at right angles to the floor while shining a flashlight into the top of each. The beams of light should be directed onto the white oak tag.

3

1. To mix colored light you will need cellophane filters in the three primary colors – green, red, and blue.

3. Find out how to make new colors by positioning the three lights in such a way as to produce a variety of combinations. Where the three combine, white light is produced.

3

25

PIGMENTS

Thousands of years ago, natural pigments from the earth were being used by Stone Age artists to create cave paintings. Later, plants were to provide dyes for cloth. Color in painting is not made by splitting white light. The primary colors of paint are magenta, cyan, and yellow (red, blue, and yellow). If you look closely at color on a printed page, you will see that it is made up of tiny dots of these colors. The primary colors of paint mix together to make black, not white like light. Pigments combine to create other colors inside the eye and brain without being mixed themselves. Pigments can be separated using chromatography.

CHROMATOGRAPHY

1. For this project, use water-based felt-tip pens or inks. You will also need blotting paper and a deep container, one-quarter full of clean water. Cut the blotting paper into long strips about 2 in wide. On each strip make a blot of color. Mark some strips with different shapes, using a different color on each.

2. Lay the strips over the edge of the container of water, with the colored mark nearest to the water. The end of each should just touch the water. Leave the bowl undisturbed for some time. The water will soak upward, due to capillary action, spreading the pigments up each strip.

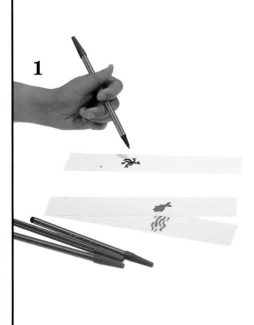

3. As the water travels up the blotting paper, the pigments in the inks begin to move also. When the pigments can travel no further, remove the strips and allow them to dry.

WHY IT WORKS

The pigments in inks travel at different speeds. As the water rises up the paper the pigments separate out in bands of color.

The primary pigments make other colors because they absorb color. Each primary color of paint absorbs one of the primary colors of light and reflects the other two. The colors are formed by subtractive mixing and are different to those created by the additive mixing of light. Pigments in paint reflect light from other sources. A white sheet of paper reflects all the light that falls on it – no subtraction takes place. A black sheet absorbs all of the light – all three primary colors are subtracted.

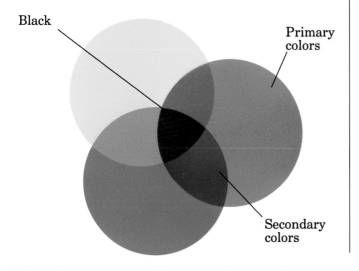

Black

Primary colors

Secondary colors

BRIGHT IDEAS

💡 Paint an Impressionist picture using dots of paint in primary colors. Stand back and look at your picture from a distance. See if the dots merge to form new colors.

💡 Adapt your main project to make a color wheel. Cut out a circle of white blotting paper, large enough to rest on top of a transparent beaker. At the center make a large dot with water-based ink or felt tip. Fill the beaker almost to the top with water and rest the circle on top. Cut a strip from the edge to the center and fold it so it hangs in the water. As the ink dissolves it will separate into its various colors to form rings.

4. Study the strips carefully. Which pigments seem to travel fastest? These colors will have traveled further up the strips. What has happened to your shapes?

4

MOVING PICTURES

Eadweard Muybridge was the first person to photograph a horse in full gallop, using 12 cameras in sequence. Moving pictures are only possible because of the nature of the human eye. In fact, they deceive the eye because each picture is really a "still" photograph. If these photographs pass in front of the eyes fast enough, there seems to be continuous movement. Cartoon films (animation) use the same technique. "Snow White and the Seven Dwarfs," pictured left, is a famous animated film by Walt Disney. A popular forerunner of the movies was the praxinoscope. You can make your own praxinoscope and watch your drawings come to life.

You can trace this design to make your own praxinoscope.

Use bright colors to illustrate your praxinoscope.

Design your own pictures, making sure each one moves postion slightly.

Place a board underneath your praxinoscope before cutting the slits. Ask an adult to help.

Why It Works

Moving pictures depend upon illusion. A moving film is a series of still pictures seen one after the other at high speed. Every image remains in the eye of the viewer for 1/10 of a second after it has left the screen. As the next image appears, it merges with the picture before it, producing the illusion of continuous movement. Usually, 24 pictures or frames are taken every second by a movie camera. As light enters the movie camera, a lens focuses an image onto one frame of the unexposed film. After it has been exposed, the film is drawn through the camera, exposing the next frame. The light entering the camera is also bent into the eyepiece using a prism, where the image can be viewed by the operator.

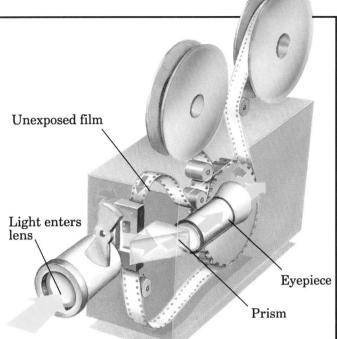

Unexposed film

Light enters lens

Eyepiece

Prism

A Parrot Praxinoscope

1

1. Draw a circle of 6 inches in diameter. On the outside draw a series of images at different stages of movement. Mark out where the slits should be cut as shown.

2. Color the images and the background, then cut out the circle. Use a craft knife and ruler to cut out the viewing strips. Ask for adult help.

2

3. Pierce the center of the cardboard with a nail and push it through to the back. Slide a washer and then a cork onto the nail. This will be your handle.

3

4. Ask a friend to hold a flat mirror in front of you so that the praxinoscope is reflected back to your eyes. Hold the cork and rotate the cardboard. View the parrots in flight through the viewing slits. Make sure that you rotate the circle in the right direction or the parrots will fly backward.

4

Bright Ideas

Make your own cartoon movie with a tin lid and a bamboo stick. Make a spinning top with the lid and stick, then attach a paper strip of about 20 drawings to the outside edge. To create a sense of movement, draw the same figure in a slightly different position each time. Ask a friend to spin the lid while you view the "movie" through a pinhole in a sheet of cardboard.

Make a flip book. A different moving picture can be made by drawing a face onto two sides of a folded sheet of paper. The face on the top "page" should not be smiling. The same face on the bottom "page" should be smiling. Hold the paper at the fold and roll the top page around a pencil. Now move the pencil quickly back and forth over the smiling face underneath to make the smile "move."

CONCENTRATED LIGHT

Lasers produce a beam of pure light in which the waves are all identical. The light is very concentrated and can be used in many ways. You may have a compact disc player. These contain a laser beam which reads the disc. Surgical lasers are used in hospitals, for example, to carry out delicate eye operations. You may have seen a hologram on a credit card. These are 3-D photographs produced using laser light. Light can also travel along fibers of glass to carry images or sounds. This is known as fiber optics. Optical fibers can carry telephone messages long distances. A fiber-optic endoscope enables a doctor to look inside a patient's body.

WHY IT WORKS

The light produced by a laser is all of the same wavelength. Each color of white light has a different wavelength. In ordinary light, the waves travel in different directions. In laser light, the waves are all in step. A laser can be concentrated onto a tiny point. It can be used for eye surgery and it can cut metal.

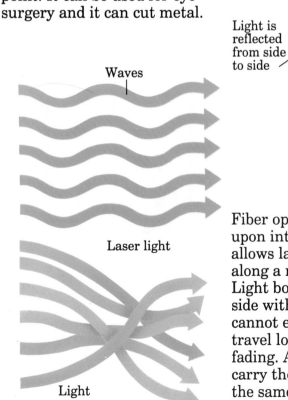

Waves

Laser light

Light

Light is reflected from side to side

Glass fiber

Light

Fiber optic devices depend upon internal reflection that allows laser light to pass along a narrow glass fiber. Light bounces from side to side within the fiber and cannot escape. The light can travel long distances without fading. A fiber-optic cable can carry thousands of signals at the same time at high speed.

BRIGHT IDEAS

Holograms are often seen today – keep a record of those you see. Why are they used on credit cards?

Next time you are in a supermarket, at the checkout, observe how each item is checked off. Some shops use lasers that produce infrared rays similar to light rays. The laser reads the bar code on each item, so that a beam reflects from it, sending a signal to a computer. The computer sends the price back to the checkout and records the item sold.

Find out about the many uses of lasers – they are used by dentists and surgeons. Laser light is often used to create special effects to entertain. You may have seen a laser show.

A STREAM OF LIGHT

1. First paint a transparent plastic bottle black and then cut off the top. With a drawing pin, make one pinhole near the bottom of the bottle. On the other side of the bottle, opposite the pinhole, scrape away a small area of paint, sufficient to allow light to pass through. Now stand the bottle in a large flat glass dish, with the pinhole facing inward.

2. Place the dish in a darkened room and half fill the bottle with water. Shine a flashlight through the bottle as shown and place your finger in the stream of water that will emerge from the pinhole. You should be able to see a spot of light on your finger. The jet of water acts like the glass fiber of an optic cable. The light from the flashlight is bounced back and forth along the stream of water, and concentrated into a small spot on your finger.

2

Scientific Terms

CONCAVE Curving inward like the inside of a spoon.
CONVEX Curving outward like the outside of a spoon.
ECLIPSE An eclipse occurs when one planet stops sunlight from reaching another.
FIBER OPTICS A way of sending light along very thin glass fibers.
FOCUS The point at which light rays come together to form a sharp, clear image.
HOLOGRAM A three-dimensional picture produced by a laser.

IMAGE The "picture" of an object produced by a mirror or lens.
LASER Stands for Light Amplification by Stimulated Emission of Radiation. A concentrated beam of light of one wavelength.
PHOTON The smallest particle of light energy.
PIGMENT A substance that gives color to a plant or animal cell. Can be used to color paints or dyes.
PRISM A transparent block of glass, used to bend light

and separate the colors in visible light.
REFLECTION Bouncing back of light from a surface.
REFRACTION Bending of light when it passes from one transparent substance to another.
RETINA Layer of cells at the back of the eye that is sensitive to light.
WAVELENGTH The length between two waves. Each type of light and the colors that make up visible light have different wavelengths.

Index

bioethanol 10

cameras 13, 29
cartoon movies 28, 29
chlorophyll 10, 11
chromatography 26-7
colors 22, 24-7
concave lenses 18, 21
concave mirrors 16, 17, 21
cones 24
convex lenses 18, 19, 20, 21
convex mirrors 17

eclipses 6, 7
endoscopes 30
eyes 12-13, 24, 28

fiber optics 30
fire 3
flip books 29

Galileo Galilei 20
glass 8

Herschel, Sir William 16
holograms 30

infrared rays 8, 30

kaleidoscopes 15

lasers 30
lenses 12, 13, 18, 19, 20-1
light rays 6, 8, 13, 14, 18, 20, 22
light waves 6, 18, 30
luminous objects 8

magnifying glasses 17, 19, 21
microscopes 18-19
mirrors 14, 15, 16-17, 18
moon 6, 7, 8, 16, 17
moving pictures 28-9

Newton, Sir Isaac 16, 22
nonluminous objects 8

opaque objects 7, 8
optic nerves 12
optical illusions 13

penumbras 7
periscopes 14-15, 22
photons 6
photograph 28
photosynthesis 10, 11
phototropism 11
pigments 26-7
pinhole cameras 13
plants 3, 10, 11
praxinoscopes 28, 29

primary colors 24, 25, 26, 27
prisms 14, 22, 29

rainbows 8, 22-3
reflection 14-15, 24, 27, 30
refracting telescopes 20, 21
refraction 18-19, 22

safety rules 4
secondary colors 24
shadows 6-7
sight 12, 13, 14, 15, 24
spectrum 22-3, 24
speed of light 8
stained glass 8
sun 3, 8, 10, 17
sundials 6, 7
sunlight 3, 8, 10-11

telescopes 16-17, 20, 21
televisions 24
translucent objects 8
transparent objects 8

ultraviolet rays 8
umbras 7

water 18, 19, 22
wavelengths 8, 22, 24, 30
white light 8, 22, 24, 25, 30